Fantastic ★ Physical ★ Science ★ Experiments

Sizzling Science Projects with Heat and Energy

Robert Gardner

Enslow Elementary
an imprint of

Enslow Publishers, Inc.
40 Industrial Road
Box 398
Berkeley Heights, NJ 07922
USA

http://www.enslow.com

Enslow Elementary, an imprint of Enslow Publishers, Inc.

Enslow Elementary® is a registered trademark of Enslow Publishers, Inc.

Library of Congress Cataloging-in-Publication Data

Gardner, Robert, 1929–
Sizzling science projects with heat and energy / Robert Gardner.
    p. cm. — (Fantastic physical science experiments)
Includes bibliographical references and index.
ISBN 0-7660-2586-1
1. Heat—Experiments—Juvenile literature. 2. Energy—Experiments—
Juvenile literature. I. Title.
QC256.G37 2006
536—dc22

                                                              2005033755

Printed in the United States of America

10 9 8 7 6 5 4 3 2 1

To Our Readers: We have done our best to make sure all Internet Addresses
in this book were active and appropriate when we went to press. However, the
author and the publisher have no control over and assume no liability for the
material available on those Internet sites or on other Web sites they may link to.
Any comments or suggestions can be sent by e-mail to comments@enslow.com
or to the address on the back cover.

Illustration credits: Tom LaBaff

Cover illustration: Tom LaBaff

Contents

(Experiments with a 🎀 symbol feature **Ideas for Your Science Fair**.)

Introduction

We need energy to live. Our energy comes from food we eat. Energy is stored in food. The main source of all food energy is sunlight. It comes from the atomic energy released when hydrogen forms helium inside the sun.

Another kind of energy is stored in the batteries that light a flashlight. Energy is also stored in every spring that's stretched. Heat is also a kind of energy.

As you will discover, there are many kinds of energy. Energy can change from one kind to another, but every kind of energy can be changed to heat. In fact, some of the energy stored in food changes to heat inside you. It keeps you warm.

You can learn much more about heat and other kinds of energy. Just do the experiments in this book.

Entering a Science Fair

Most of the experiments in this book (those marked with a 🏵 symbol) are followed by ideas for science fair projects. Judges at science fairs like experiments that are creative. So do not simply copy an experiment from this book. Expand on one of the ideas suggested, or think of a project of your own. Choose a topic you really like and want to know more about. Then your project will be more interesting to you. Your curiosity can lead to a creative experiment that you plan and carry out.

Before entering a science fair, read one or more of the books listed under Further Reading. They will give you helpful hints and lots of useful information about science fairs.

Safety First

To do experiments safely, always follow these rules:

❶ Do all experiments under adult supervision.

❷ Read all instructions carefully. If you have questions, check with the adult.

❸ Be serious when experimenting. Fooling around can be dangerous to you and to others.

❹ Keep the area where you work clean and organized. When you have finished, clean up and put materials away.

❺ Never experiment with electric wall outlets.

❻ When doing these experiments, use only non-mercury thermometers, such as those filled with alcohol. The liquid in some thermometers is mercury. It is dangerous to breathe mercury vapor. If you have mercury thermometers, **ask an adult** to take them to a local mercury thermometer exchange location.

1. Heat and Temperature

Heat is needed to melt ice. But will an ice cube melt faster in a small amount of hot water or in a large amount of cold water?

Let's Find Out!

1 Fill two medicine cups to the 30-mL (1-oz) line with water. Put the cups in a freezer overnight.

2 Using a measuring cup, get 30 mL (1 oz) of hot water from a faucet. Pour the water into a small (4- to 6-oz) plastic cup.

3 Get 600 mL (20 oz) of cold water from a faucet. Pour it into a 1-quart plastic container.

4 Take the two identical pieces of ice from the freezer. Pop them out of the medicine cups. Put one piece into the hot water. At the same time, put the

Things you will need:
- ✔ two 30-mL (1-oz) medicine cups
- ✔ cold and hot tap water
- ✔ a freezer
- ✔ measuring cup
- ✔ 4- or 6-oz plastic cup such as a small yogurt cup
- ✔ large (1-quart) plastic container
- ✔ 2 drinking straws

Are NOT the Same!

other piece into the cold water. Use separate straws to stir the water in both containers.

Which piece of ice melted first? Which water held more heat energy? Why did it make sense to stir the water?

30 mL hot water

ice

600 mL cold water

Heat and Temperature Are NOT

You probably found that the ice in cold water melted first. The big amount of cold water had more heat than the small amount of hot water. At first, the ice in the hot water melted fast. But after a short time, it melted very slowly. The ice had taken most of the heat from the hot water. Meanwhile, the ice in the cold water melted at a steady pace. Heat flowed slowly, but steadily, from the cold water into the ice. Like the story of the tortoise and the hare, *slow but steady wins the race.*

Stirring the water kept the ice from being surrounded by the cold melted water. Stirring kept it in touch with the warmer water you put it into.

As you can see, heat is more than temperature. Heat is spread through all of a substance. If you have more substance, you have more heat. A large amount of something at a low temperature can have more heat than a small amount of the same stuff at a high temperature.

the Same!: An Explanation

A lake of cold water holds more heat than a kettle of hot water.

Ideas for Your Science Fair

* Will ice melt faster in warm air or in cold water?
* Suppose you have a gallon of water and a pint of water, both at the same temperature. In which water will an ice cube melt faster?

2. Energy and a

Anything that is moving has motion energy. Does a ball held above the floor have energy?

Let's Find Out!

1. Hold a ball above the floor. It is not moving. Does it have any energy? Let go of the ball. What happens?

Things you will need:
- ✔ a ball, such as a tennis or golf ball
- ✔ hard floor
- ✔ scissors
- ✔ thread
- ✔ meterstick or yardstick
- ✔ heavy metal washer
- ✔ tape
- ✔ door frame

2. Use scissors to cut a piece of thread about a meter (yard) long. Tie one end to a heavy metal washer. Tape the other end to a door frame. You have made a pendulum.

3. Pull the washer to one side. Why does this give the washer energy? Let go of the washer. What happens to its energy?

Pendulum

What energy changes happen as the pendulum swings back and forth? The pendulum finally stops moving. What do you think has happened to its energy?

Energy and a Pendulum:

You do work when you pull or push an object through a distance. Doing work on an object gives it energy. You did work on the ball. You pulled the ball up a distance above the floor. You gave it stored energy. Stored energy is also called potential energy. When the ball fell, its potential energy changed to motion energy. Motion energy is called kinetic energy.

The pendulum swung back and forth. You pulled the washer to the side. This raised it higher. The work you did gave it potential energy. When you released it, it swung downward and sideways. It gained kinetic energy. Beyond the middle of its swing, it moved upward until it stopped. It gained potential energy and lost kinetic energy. Then it came back down again, repeating the cycle.

Many experiments have shown that energy is never lost or gained. But it may change from one kind to another. As the pendulum lost potential energy, it gained kinetic energy. As it lost kinetic energy, it gained potential energy. But the pendulum finally stopped. Did its energy disappear? No! The pendulum's energy

An Explanation

heated the air it bumped into by a small amount. As you will see in the next experiment, kinetic energy can be changed to heat. In fact, every kind of energy can be changed to heat.

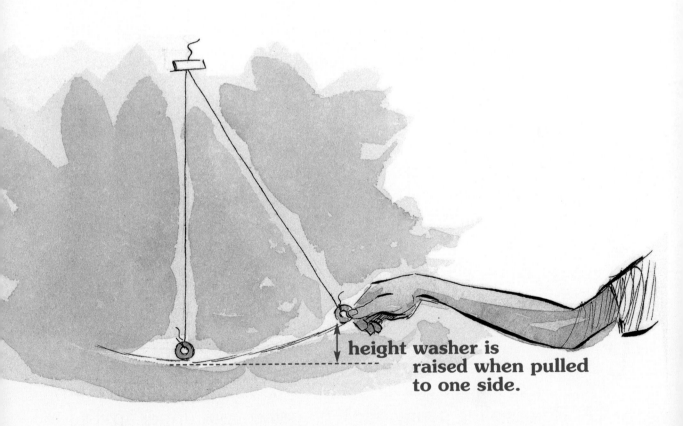

height washer is raised when pulled to one side.

3. Kinetic Energy to

You have read that all kinds of energy can be changed to heat. Can experiments show that kinetic (motion) energy can be changed to heat?

Let's Find Out!

1 Use scissors to cut a 2-inch square from a Styrofoam cup. Fold the Styrofoam square around a penny. This will help keep heat in the penny.

Things you will need:
- ✔ an adult
- ✔ scissors
- ✔ Styrofoam cup
- ✔ ruler
- ✔ a penny (preferably one minted before 1982)
- ✔ tape
- ✔ heavy piece of wood
- ✔ hammer

2 Tape the wrapped penny firmly to a heavy piece of wood.

3 **Ask an adult** to hit the covered penny hard 50 times with a hammer. The hammer has kinetic energy. Its kinetic energy is lost each time it hits the penny.

4 Remove the penny. Hold it against your upper lip. Did the penny get warmer?

Heat

Here's another way to see that kinetic energy can be changed to heat.

❺ Hold the palms of your two hands firmly together. Then move them rapidly back and forth. Do they get warmer?

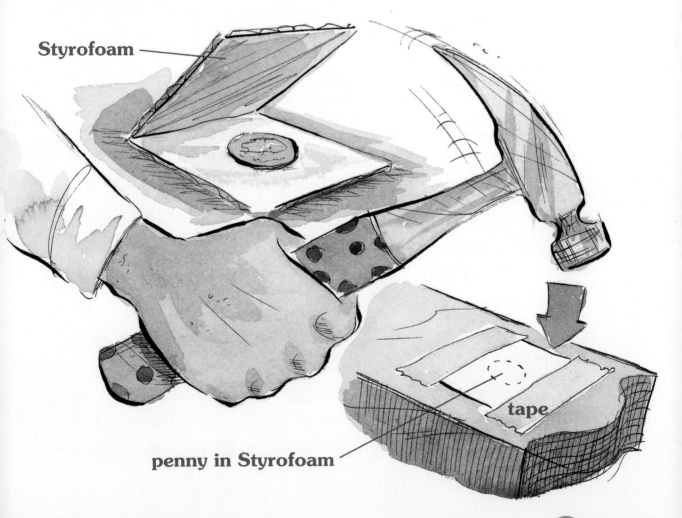

Styrofoam

penny in Styrofoam

tape

Kinetic Energy to Heat:

All matter is made of molecules. A molecule is the smallest particle of a substance that can exist. Molecules are very small. There are a billion trillion water molecules in one drop of water.

Heat is the energy of all the molecules in something. Scientists call it internal energy. We will call it heat, a more familiar word. A moving hammer has kinetic (motion) energy. When it hits something and stops, it loses its kinetic energy. But energy never just disappears. The hammer's kinetic energy changes to heat. The temperature of both the hammer and whatever it hits rises. When the hammer hit the penny, the molecules in the hammer and the penny were pushed. Work was done on them. The speed of their molecules increased. The molecules gained kinetic energy.

Temperature measures the average kinetic energy of molecules. The temperature of the penny increased. Why? Because the molecules in the penny gained kinetic energy. Work was done on them. The molecules in the penny moved faster after being pushed by the hammer.

An Explanation

The same thing happens when someone pushes you. The push makes you move. And, like a molecule, you gain kinetic energy.

Bump—and you get kinetic energy!

Bump—and molecules get more kinetic energy.

Idea for Your Science Fair

★ Do another experiment to show that the potential energy in a raised weight can be changed to heat.

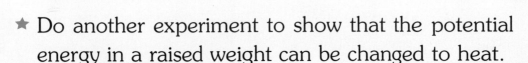

4. Elastic Potential

Energy can be stored in a stretched spring or rubber band. Such energy is called elastic potential energy (EPE). Can EPE be changed to other kinds of energy?

 Let's Find Out!

❶ Put on safety glasses. Put one end of a rubber band over the end of your thumb. Give the rubber band some EPE. Do work on it. Pull back on the other end of the rubber band.

Energy

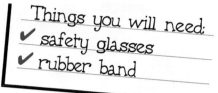

② **Be sure no one is in front of you!** Then let go of the end you pulled back. What happens to the EPE in the rubber band?

Soon the rubber band will stop. When it stops, what has happened to its kinetic energy?

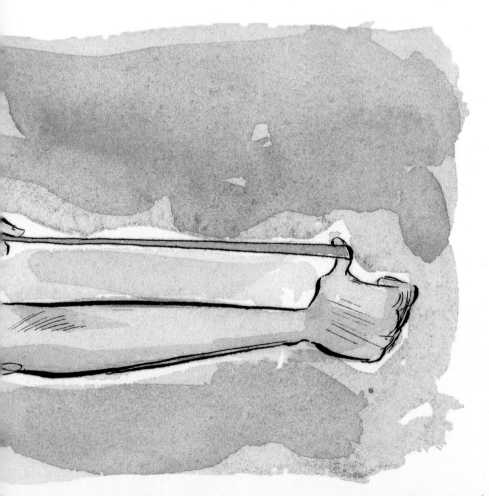

Elastic Potential Energy:

When you pulled back the rubber band, you gave it elastic potential energy (EPE). When you released the stretched rubber band, it flew off your finger. It moved at a high speed. The EPE in the rubber band was changed to kinetic (motion) energy. When the rubber band stopped, a small amount of heat was produced. The molecules in the rubber

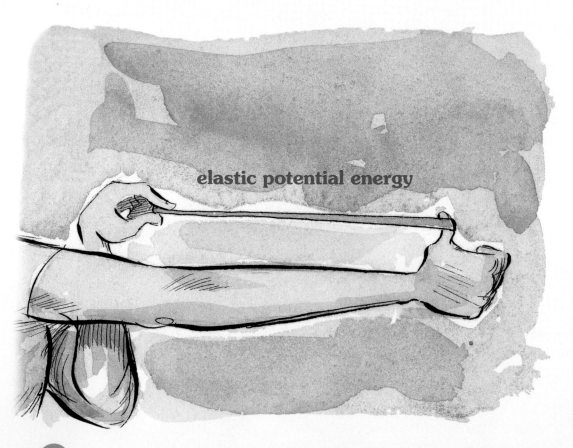

elastic potential energy

An Explanation

band were moving slightly faster than they were before the collision. So were the molecules of whatever it hit.

Idea for Your Science Fair

★ A stretched spring has EPE. How does the amount of weight hanging from a spring affect the amount it stretches? Does the stretch double when the weight doubles?

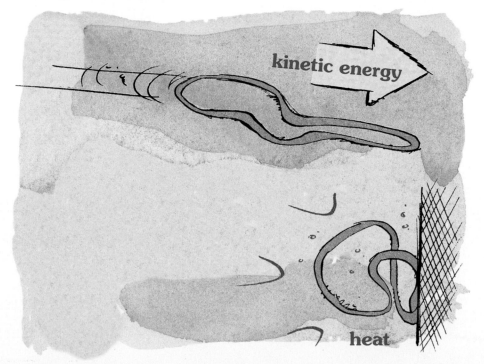

kinetic energy

heat

5. Light to Heat

I f light is energy, you should be able to change it to heat. Can you?

 Let's Find Out!

Things you will need:
- ✔ an adult
- ✔ tin can
- ✔ flat black paint
- ✔ paint brush
- ✔ 2 small alcohol thermometers with a range of about -10 to 50°C (10 to 120°F). You might borrow one from your school's science teacher.
- ✔ pencil and paper
- ✔ plastic sandwich bag
- ✔ strong rubber band
- ✔ bright sunlight (sunny window or a sunny spot outdoors)
- ✔ clock or watch
- ✔ magnifying glass
- ✔ small board
- ✔ tape

❶ **Ask an adult** to paint a tin can, inside and out, with flat black paint. Let the paint dry.

❷ Place an alcohol-based thermometer in the can. Cover the top of the can and thermometer with a plastic sandwich bag. Put a strong rubber band around the bag to make the can airtight. Write down the temperature inside the can.

❸ Place the can in bright sunlight. A sunny window will do.

❹ After 30 minutes, what is the air temperature in the

can? Write it down. Did the temperature rise? Did the air gain heat? Does the temperature continue to rise? If it does, will it finally stop rising?

⑤ **Have an adult** hold a magnifying glass near a small board in bright sunlight. The magnifier can "pull" light together and make a tiny circle of bright light on the board. Tape a thermometer to the board. Let the spot of light shine on the thermometer bulb. Does the temperature rise? Don't let it rise more than 10 degrees.

Can light be changed to heat?

Light to Heat:

Suppose you put a shiny unpainted can and the black one next to each other in sunlight. You would see the black can reflecting less light than the shiny one. The reason is that black soaks up sunlight. It changes light to heat. Then the heat passes from the can to the air in the can. This raises the air temperature. Because light is a kind of energy, it can be changed to heat. In fact, sunlight keeps Earth's surface warm. Without the sun's energy, Earth's surface would be frozen and lifeless.

The temperature inside the can will finally stop rising. This happens when the air and can lose as much heat to the cooler air as they gain from the light.

A magnifying glass can focus (bend together) sunlight. The light comes together in a small, bright spot of light. That light can be focused on the liquid in the thermometer bulb. Some of the energy heats the liquid. The kinetic energy of the liquid molecules increases; the liquid's temperature rises. Liquids expand when heated. The expanding liquid goes up the narrow opening at the top of the bulb. We see this as a rise in temperature.

An Explanation

thermometer

HEAT OUT

HEAT IN

Heat in = Heat out
(no temperature change)

Ideas for Your Science Fair

★ Build a solar heater. Use it to help heat a room with a south-facing window.

★ Do experiments to see which colors are best for changing light to heat.

6. Electric Energy to

A battery has a positive (+) end and a negative (–) end. When the ends are connected, electric charges flow from the negative end to the positive end. The charges have electric energy. The electric energy can be changed to light in a bulb. How can you get the charges to go through the bulb?

Let's Begin!

❶ Find a bare copper wire, a D-cell battery, and a flashlight bulb. Ask a friend to help you. You may need an extra pair of hands.

Things you will need:
✔ bare copper
   wire about 8
   inches long
✔ D-cell battery
   (1.5 volt)
✔ incandescent
   flashlight bulb
   rated 1.5-6 volts
✔ a friend

❷ Make the bulb light using just the wire, battery, and bulb. In how many different ways can you make the bulb light?

❸ Are there special places the wire must touch the bulb?

❹ Are there special places the wire must touch the battery?

Light

5 What happens to the electric energy as charges flow through the bulb?

Electric Energy to Light:

There are chemicals inside a battery. The chemicals form electric charges. The charges have electric energy. When the two ends of a battery are connected, electric charges move from the negative end to the positive end of the battery. Along the way, the charges can go through a bulb's filament (the thin wire that glows). In the filament, some electric energy is changed to light.

The drawings show several ways to light the bulb using one wire and a battery. You may find other

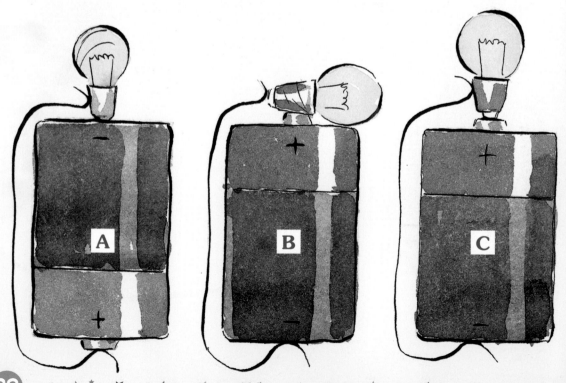

An Explanation

ways. Charge has to flow from one end of the battery to the other through metal. Certain metal things must be touched by other metal things. These things are the ends of the battery, the metal side of the bulb, and the metal tab at the bottom of the bulb.

To make the bulb light, charges must go through the bulb's filament. Wires connect the filament to the metal tab at the bulb's base and to the metal side of the bulb. (See the drawing.) As charges flow through the filament, some electric energy changes to light.

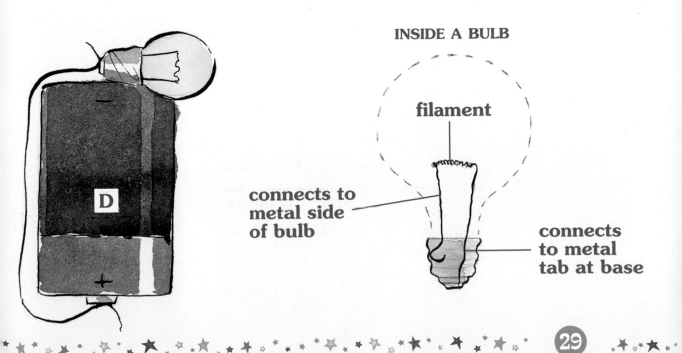

INSIDE A BULB

filament

connects to metal side of bulb

connects to metal tab at base

D

7. Electric Energy to

I s light the only kind of energy coming from a light bulb?

 Let's Find Out!

Things you will need:
- ✔ 30-mL (1-oz) medicine cup
- ✔ cold water
- ✔ 7-oz Styrofoam cup
- ✔ small alcohol thermometer with a range of about -10 to 50°C (10 to 120°F). You might borrow one from your school's science teacher.
- ✔ pencil and paper
- ✔ miniature 6.3-V lightbulb
- ✔ bulb holder
- ✔ 2 insulated wires with alligator clips on both ends
- ✔ 6-V lantern battery
- ✔ clock or watch

Electrical materials can be purchased at an electronics store.

❶ Pour 30 mL (1 oz) of cold water (1 to 2 degrees below room temperature) into an insulated (Styrofoam) cup. Put an alcohol thermometer in the water. When the temperature stops changing, write it down.

❷ Put a miniature 6.3-V flashlight bulb into a bulb holder. Clip an insulated wire to each metal lead on the bulb holder. Put the bulb under the water in the Styrofoam cup. Be sure the two wires don't touch one another.

❸ Clip the other ends of the two wires to the terminals

Light and Heat?

of a 6-V lantern battery as shown. You have made an electric circuit. The bulb should glow brightly under the water.

4 Let electricity flow through the glowing bulb for 15 minutes. Then disconnect the wires. Stir the water with the thermometer. Write down the final temperature of the water.

Was any electric energy changed to light? Was any electric energy changed to heat?

Is any electric energy in your house changed to light? Is any of that electric energy changed to heat?

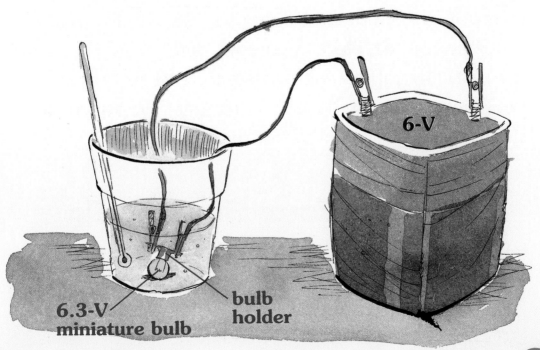

6-V

6.3-V
miniature bulb

bulb
holder

Electric Energy to Light

In this experiment, you found that electric energy was changed to both light and heat. Suppose you had covered the bulb with aluminum foil. Then the light could not have escaped. All the electric energy would have been changed to heat.

There is potential (stored) energy in the chemicals inside the battery. When the battery ends are connected, some of that stored energy becomes electric energy. Electric charges carry the energy from one battery end to the other. Along the way, the electric energy may be changed to other kinds of energy. Light and heat are two such kinds of energy.

Suppose the electric charges had gone through an electric motor instead of a lightbulb. Then some of the electric energy would have been changed to kinetic (motion) energy in the spinning motor.

Ideas for Your Science Fair

★ Wrap the glass part of the bulb with aluminum foil. Repeat the experiment. Do you notice less light and more heat?

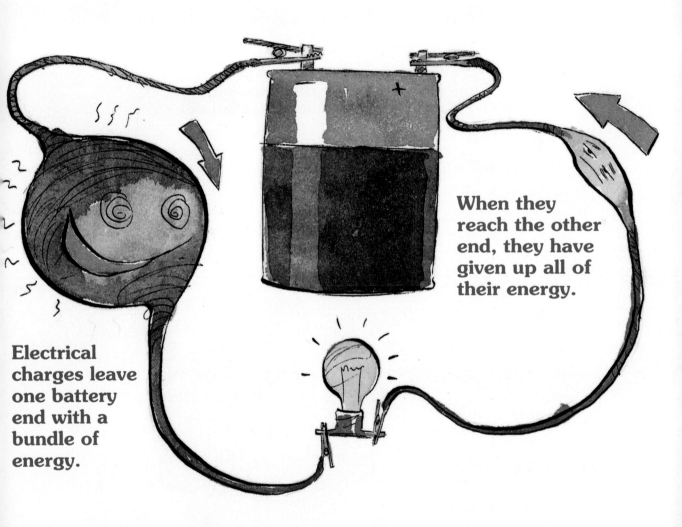

When they reach the other end, they have given up all of their energy.

Electrical charges leave one battery end with a bundle of energy.

★ Place the bulb in black water. To blacken the water, add black ink or red, blue, and green food coloring. Repeat the experiment. Will you notice more heat and less light?

8. Light Energy to and

Sunlight is a free source of energy. Can sunlight be changed to electric energy?

 Let's Find Out!

Things you will need:
- ✔ 2 insulated wires with alligator clips on both ends
- ✔ D-cell battery
- ✔ 2- to 3-volt miniature lightbulb
- ✔ bulb holder
- ✔ toy electric motor (available from an electronics or toy store)
- ✔ solar (photovoltaic) cell that is connected to a toy motor (available from an electronics or toy store)
- ✔ bright sunlight
- ✔ glass window facing the sun

❶ Find two insulated wires with alligator clips on both ends. Connect the + and – ends of a D-cell battery to a miniature lightbulb in a bulb holder as shown. As you can see, electric energy is changed to light energy.

❷ Use the same wires to connect the leads of a toy motor to the + and – ends of a D-cell battery. As you can see, electric energy turns the motor. Some electric energy is changed to kinetic (motion) energy in the motor. What other kind of energy might also be found in the motor?

from Electric Energy

3 Get a toy motor that is connected to a solar cell. Take the solar cell and motor outside into bright sunlight. Turn the cell so that it directly faces the sun. Does the motor turn? Can light energy be changed to electric energy?

4 Take the solar cell and motor inside. Hold them in sunlight that has passed through a glass window. Does the solar cell make the motor turn? If the motor doesn't turn, can you explain why it doesn't?

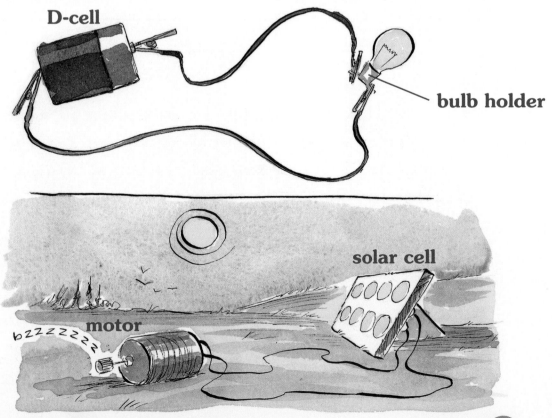

D-cell

bulb holder

solar cell

motor

bzzzzzzzz

As you have learned, electric energy can be changed to light. In this experiment, you discovered that light can be changed to electric energy. Electric energy is needed to make a motor turn. You connected a motor to a solar cell. When they were placed in sunlight, the motor turned.

Solar cells change light energy to electric energy. Solar cells are made mostly of silicon. Light energizes the charges in the silicon. This causes them to move along wires. The solar cell acts like a battery.

There are no electric power lines near satellites in space. There are none in places where very few people live. In many such places, solar cells are used to make electric energy. Solar cells are expensive. For their price, they can't compete with other ways of making electric energy. And they are not useful in places where there is little sunshine. But the cost of solar cells is decreasing. They may be used more in the future.

The solar cell may not have made the motor turn when you took it inside. Glass windows absorb some solar energy. The solar cell may have needed more

Electrical Energy: An Explanation

light. It may not have made enough electric energy to turn the motor.

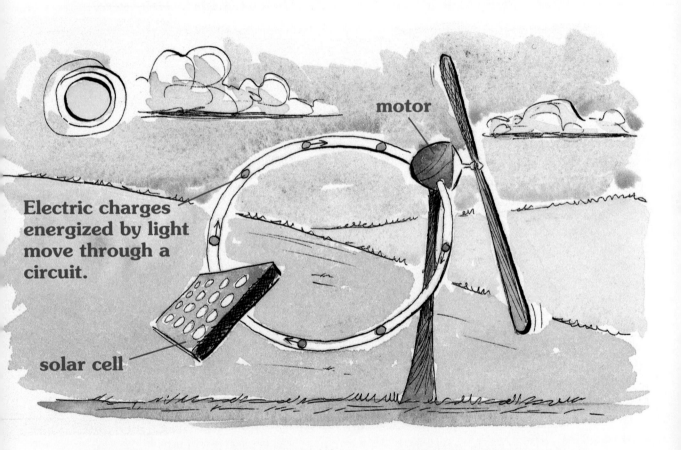

motor

Electric charges energized by light move through a circuit.

solar cell

Idea for Your Science Fair

★ Does the angle at which light hits the solar cell affect the amount of electric energy from the solar cell?

9. Keeping Heat with

Heat flows from warm objects to cold ones. To save energy, builders put insulation in the walls and ceilings of homes. Insulation slows the flow of heat. What makes a good insulator?

 Let's Find Out!

Things you will need:
- ✓ scissors
- ✓ 2 Styrofoam cups
- ✓ drinking glass, plastic cup, and metal can with covers of the same materials
- ✓ very hot tap water
- ✓ pitcher
- ✓ small alcohol thermometer with a range of about -10 to 50°C (10 to 120°F). You might borrow one from your school's science teacher.
- ✓ pencil and paper
- ✓ measuring cup
- ✓ clock or watch
- ✓ 4 identical ice cubes

❶ Using scissors, cut off the top quarter of a Styrofoam cup.

❷ Line up a metal can, plastic cup, drinking glass, and a whole Styrofoam cup. To each, add a cover made of the same material—the metal top of a larger can, a plastic lid, a glass plate, the bottom of the cut-off Styrofoam cup.

❸ Put 1 liter (1 quart) of very hot tap water in a pitcher. Measure and write down the water's temperature. Using a measuring cup, quickly

Insulation

pour 150 mL (5 oz) of the hot water into each container. Cover the containers.

4 Wait 30 minutes. Then quickly measure the water temperature in each container. Write them down. In which container was the water temperature highest? Which container was the best insulator?

5 Dry the containers. Let them cool to room temperature.

6 Get four identical ice cubes. Put one in each container. Put on the covers. Predict the container in which ice will melt slowest. Were you right?

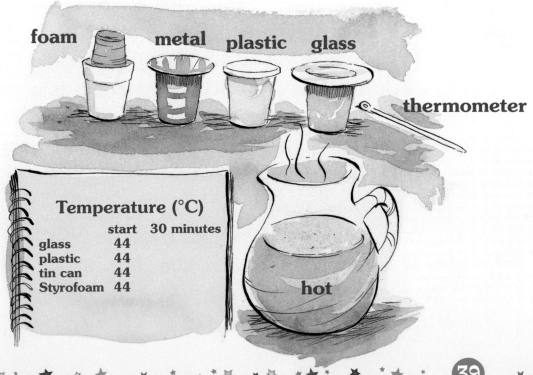

foam   metal   plastic   glass

thermometer

Temperature (°C)		
	start	30 minutes
glass	44	
plastic	44	
tin can	44	
Styrofoam	44	

hot

Heat is the kinetic (motion) energy of molecules. Hotter (faster) molecules bump into colder (slower) molecules. When they do, they give some of their energy to the slower molecules. In this way, heat flows from warm objects to cooler ones. Insulation slows this process. Most insulation, such as Styrofoam, contains lots of air spaces. The molecules in air are far apart. Because they are far apart, the molecules bump into each other less often. As a result, heat flows slowly through insulation. It flows faster through solid materials such as metals and glass.

You probably found the water temperature was highest in the Styrofoam cup. Styrofoam is a better insulator than glass, plastic, or metals. The "foam" part of Styrofoam indicates that it contains tiny air spaces. These air spaces slow the flow of heat to the cooler air in the room.

You probably predicted that ice would melt slowest inside the Styrofoam cup. The tiny air spaces in the Styrofoam slowed the flow of the heat from the warm room air to the ice.

Insulation: An Explanation

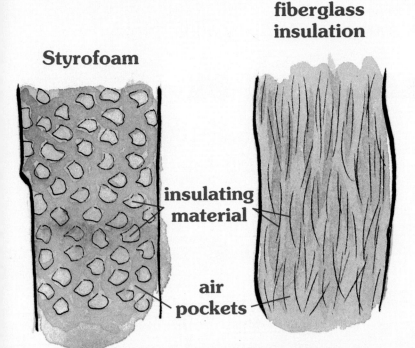

Styrofoam

fiberglass insulation

down comforter

insulating material

air pockets

Insulation has many air pockets.

Ideas for Your Science Fair

★ Does the thickness of Styrofoam affect its ability to insulate?

★ What other materials are good insulators?

★ How can you best insulate an ice cube—to keep it longest in a warm room?

★ Does heat move faster through some solids than through others?

10. How Cold Can Ice

How cold can you make water by adding ice?

 Let's Find Out!

Things you will need:
- ✔ measuring cup
- ✔ tap water
- ✔ 8-oz plastic container (such as a yogurt cup)
- ✔ small alcohol thermometer with a range of about −10 to 50°C (10 to 120°F). You might borrow one from your school's science teacher.
- ✔ pencil and paper
- ✔ plastic pail filled with crushed ice or snow (snow is ice crystals)
- ✔ medicine cup (30 mL, or 1 oz)

1. Add about 100 mL (3½ oz) of tap water to an 8-oz plastic container. Measure the water temperature with a thermometer. Write it down.

2. Fill a pail with crushed ice or snow. Add a medicine-cupful (30 mL, or 1 oz) of the crushed ice or snow to the water. Stir with the thermometer. How cold is the water now?

3. Add another medicine-cupful of ice or snow. How cold is the water now?

4. Continue to add snow or crushed ice to the water.

Make Water?

Keep writing down the temperature. How cold can you make the water?

5 Suppose you put the thermometer into the pail of ice or snow. What do you think the temperature will be? Try it! Were you right?

1 oz crushed ice

How Cold Can Ice Make

You probably found that you could not get the temperature below 0°C, or 32°F. (Your thermometer might have read a degree or two above or below 0 or 32. Inexpensive thermometers are not very accurate.) No matter how much ice or snow you added, the temperature didn't change. It stayed at 0° on the Celsius scale or 32° on the Fahrenheit scale. Why? Because ice, no matter how much, melts at 0°C (32°F). The temperature will stay at the melting temperature as long as there is ice. (The freezing and melting temperature of water is the same: 0°C, or 32°F).

Once all the ice has melted, the temperature will rise above 0°C (32°F). To get water below 0°C, put it in a freezer. After all the water has changed to ice, the temperature will slowly fall. It will fall to the temperature of the freezer.

Water?: An Explanation

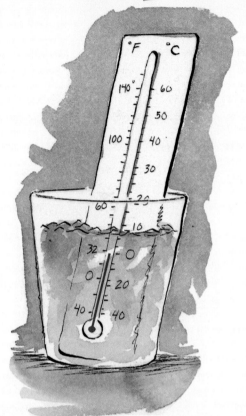

Ideas for Your Science Fair

★ Do experiments to show that the melting temperature of water is the same as its freezing temperature.

★ Measure the time it takes to melt an ice cube in air. Then measure the time it takes to raise the temperature of the melted ice by one degree. Use these times to show that it takes a lot more heat to melt the ice than it does to raise the temperature of the melted ice by one degree.

Words to Know

elastic potential energy (EPE)—The energy stored in anything that is stretched or compressed, such as a spring or a rubber ball.

electrical energy—The energy in electric charges. The energy may come from the chemicals in a battery.

freezing temperature—The temperature at which a substance changes from a liquid to a solid. For water, this temperature is 0°C, or 32°F. The freezing and melting temperatures of a substance, such as water, are the same.

heat—A kind of energy; the total energy of the molecules in a substance, more properly known as internal energy.

insulation—A material that slows the transfer of heat from a warm place to a colder place.

kinetic energy—The energy of motion. Any moving thing has kinetic energy.

light—A kind of energy released by the sun and other bright things such as electric lightbulbs.

pendulum—A weight at the end of a string or other support that swings back and forth, alternating between potential and kinetic energy.

potential energy—Stored energy. A weight sitting on a shelf has potential energy because it can do work or gain kinetic energy if it falls.

solar cell—A device that can change sunlight to electric energy.

temperature—A measure of the "hotness" of something; the average kinetic energy of the molecules of a substance.

thermometer—A device that measures temperature.

Further Reading

Books

Bochinski, Julianne Blair. *The Complete Workbook for Science Fair Projects.* New York: John Wiley and Sons, 2004.

Bradley, Kimberly Brubaker. *Energy Makes Things Happen.* New York: HarperCollins Publishers, Inc. 2003.

Dispezio, Michael A. *Super Sensational Science Fair Projects.* New York: Sterling Publishing, 2002.

Gardner, Robert. *Really Hot Science Projects with Temperature: How Hot Is It? How Cold Is It?* Berkeley Heights, N.J.: Enslow Publishers, Inc., 2003.

Kauw, Darlene. *Heat.* New York: Crabtree Publishing Company, 2002.

Knapp, Brian J. *Keeping Warm and Cool.* Danbury, Conn.: Grolier Educational, 2003.

Parker, Steve. *Energy.* Milwaukee: Garth Stevens Publishers, 2004.

Searle, Bobbie. *Heat and Energy.* Brookfield, Conn.: Copper Beech Books, 2001.

Tocci, Salvadore. *Experiments with Heat.* Danbury, Conn.: Children's Press, 2002.

Internet Addresses

Kennesaw State University. *Energy—Heat, Sound, Light.* © 2004. <http://edtech.kennesaw.edu/web/heatener.html>

MathMol. *Measuring Energy.* © 1996. <http://www.nyu.edu/pages/mathmol/textbook/measureenergy.html>

Weblearning. *Heat, Light, and Motion.* © 2004. <http://www.thetech.org/exhibits/online/topics/11a.html>

Index

3/0

WITHDRAWN

4/11 2/07